You know what I am going to say
even before I say it, LORD.
You go before me and follow me.
You place your hand of blessing on my head.
Such knowledge is too wonderful for me,
too great for me to understand!

I can never escape from your Spirit!
I can never get away from your presence!
If I go up to heaven, you are there;
if I go down to the grave, you are there.
If I ride the wings of the morning,
if I dwell by the farthest oceans,
even there your hand will guide me,
and your strength will support me.

Psalm 139:1–10
New Living Translation

God cares for you

When I consider your heavens,
the work of your fingers,
the moon and the stars,
which you have set in place,
what is mankind that you are mindful of them,
human beings that you care for them?
You have made them a little lower than the angels
and crowned them with glory and honour.
You made them rulers over the works of your hands;
you put everything under their feet...

Psalm 8:3-6
New International Version

He is our God; we are the people he cares for,
the flock for which he provides.

Psalm 95:7
Good News Translation

7

You belong to God

The earth is the LORD's, and everything in it.
The world and all its people belong to him.
For he laid the earth's foundation on the seas
and built it on the ocean depths.
Who may climb the mountain of the LORD?
Who may stand in his holy place?
Only those whose hands and hearts are pure,
who do not worship idols
and never tell lies.
They will receive the LORD's blessing
and have a right relationship with God their saviour.

Psalm 24:1–5
New Living Translation

God has good plans for you

You bless all of those
who trust you, LORD,
and refuse to worship idols
or follow false gods.

Midwinter Mist

You, LORD God, have done
many things,
and you have planned
marvellous things for us.
No one is like you!
I would never be able to tell
all you have done.

Psalm 40:4–5
Contemporary English Version

11

God will guide you

The LORD is my shepherd;
I have everything I need.
He lets me rest in fields of green grass
and leads me to quiet pools
of fresh water.
He gives me new strength.
He guides me in the right paths,
as he has promised.
...
I know that your goodness and love
will be with me all my life;
and your house will be my home
as long as I live.

Psalm 23:1–3, 6
Good News Translation

For you are my rock and my fortress,
therefore for your name's sake lead me and guide me.

Psalm 31:3
World English Bible

13

God watches
over you

The LORD watches over you –
the LORD is your shade at your right hand;
the sun will not harm you by day,
nor the moon by night.

The LORD will keep you from all harm –
he will watch over your life;
the LORD will watch over your coming and going
both now and for evermore.

Psalm 121:5-8
New International Version

Mont Saint-Michel, Normandy

16

God's angels will protect you

Whoever goes to the LORD for safety,
whoever remains under the protection
of the Almighty, can say to him,
"You are my defender and protector.
You are my God; in you I trust."...
He will cover you with his wings;
you will be safe in his care;
his faithfulness will protect and defend you.

Psalm 91:1–2, 4
Good News Translation

God will command his angels to protect you
wherever you go.

Psalm 91:11
Contemporary English Version

God hears your prayers

I praise you, LORD,
for answering my prayers.
You are my strong shield,
and I trust you completely.

Psalm 28:6–7
Contemporary English Version

I asked the LORD for help,
and he saved me
from all my fears.
Keep your eyes on the LORD!
You will shine like the sun
and never blush with shame.
I was a nobody,
but I prayed,
and the LORD saved me
from all my troubles.
...
The LORD hears his people when they call
to him for help.
He rescues them from all their troubles.

Psalm 34:4-6, 17
Contemporary English Version and New Living Translation

19

God's love for you
will last forever

Sing to the LORD, all the world!
Worship the LORD with joy;
come before him with happy songs!

Acknowledge that the LORD is God.
He made us, and we belong to him;
we are his people, we are his flock.
Enter the Temple gates with thanksgiving;
go into its courts with praise.
Give thanks to him and praise him.
The LORD is good; his love is eternal

and his faithfulness lasts forever.

Psalm: 100:1-5
Good News Translation

In the Valley

You can rely on God

The LORD is my rock, my fortress
and my deliverer;
my God is my rock, in whom I take refuge,
my shield and the horn of my salvation,
my stronghold.
I called to the LORD, who is worthy of praise,
and I have been saved from my enemies.

As for God, his way is perfect:
the LORD's word is flawless;
he shields all who take refuge in him.
For who is God besides the LORD?
And who is the Rock except our God?
It is God who arms me with strength
and keeps my way secure.

Psalm 18:2-3, 30-32
New International Version

Great Falls, Virginia, USA

God is faithful

You, LORD God,
are my mighty rock
and my fortress.
Lead me and guide me,
so that your name
will be honored.
Protect me from hidden traps
and keep me safe.
You are faithful, and I trust you
because you rescued me.

Psalm 31:3-5
Contemporary English Version

Your unfailing love, O LORD, is as vast as the heavens;
your faithfulness reaches beyond the clouds.
Your righteousness is like the mighty mountains,
your justice like the ocean depths.

Psalm 36:5-6
New Living Translation

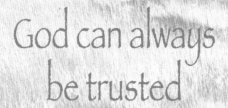

God can always be trusted

My soul finds rest in God alone;
my salvation comes from him.
He alone is my rock and my salvation;
he is my fortress, I shall never be shaken.

My salvation and my honour depend on God;
he is my mighty rock, my refuge.

Trust in him at all times, O people;
pour out your hearts to him,
for God is our refuge.

Psalm 62:1–2, 7–8
New International Version

LORD God All-Powerful,

you bless everyone who trusts you.

Psalm 84:12
Contemporary English Version

God created our world

The heavens proclaim the glory of God.
The skies display his craftsmanship.
Day after day they continue to speak;
night after night they make him known.
They speak without a sound or word;
their voice is never heard.
Yet their message has gone throughout the earth,
and their words to all the world.

Psalm 19:1–4
New Living Translation

May the LORD who created the heavens
and the earth
give you his blessing.

Psalm 115:15
Contemporary English Version

God provides a
splendid harvest

You care for the land and water it;
you enrich it abundantly.
The streams of God are filled with water
to provide the people with corn,
for so you have ordained it.
You drench its furrows and level its ridges;
you soften it with showers and bless its crops.
You crown the year with your bounty,
and your carts overflow with abundance.
The grasslands of the desert overflow;
the hills are clothed with gladness.
The meadows are covered with flocks
and the valleys are mantled with corn;
they shout for joy and sing.

Psalm 65:9–13
New International Version

The land yields its harvest;
God, our God, blesses us.

Psalm 67:6
New International Version

God provides
generously for us

With all my heart I praise the LORD,
and with all that I am I praise his holy name!
With all my heart I praise the LORD!
I will never forget how kind he has been.
The LORD forgives our sins, heals us when we are sick,
and protects us from death.
His kindness and love are a crown on our heads.
Each day that we live, he provides for our needs
and gives us the strength of a young eagle.

Psalm 103:1–5
Contemporary English Version

33

God forgives those who turn to him

Our God, you bless everyone
whose sins you forgive
and wipe away.
You bless them by saying,
"You told me your sins,
without trying to hide them,
and now I forgive you."

Psalm 32:1–2
Contemporary English Version

Evening Glow

34

As high as the sky is above the earth,
so great is his love for those who honour him.
As far as the east is from the west,
so far does he remove our sins from us.

Psalm 103:11-12
Good News Translation

Pile your troubles on GOD's shoulders
— he'll carry your load,
he'll help you out.

Psalm 55:22–23
The Message

When they call on me, I will answer;
I will be with them in trouble.
I will rescue and honour them.

Psalm 91:15
New Living Translation

I took my troubles to the LORD;
I cried out to him, and he answered my prayer.

Psalm 120:1
New Living Translation

Horsey, Norfolk

37

When life is tough,
God is our refuge

God is our refuge and strength,
a very present help in trouble.
Therefore we won't be afraid, though the earth changes,
though the mountains are shaken into the heart of the
seas; though its waters roar and are troubled,
though the mountains tremble with their swelling.

"Be still, and know that I am God.
I will be exalted among the nations.
I will be exalted in the earth."

Psalm 46:1–3, 10
World English Bible

Blessed are all those who take refuge in him.

Psalm 2:12

When we are afraid, God is with us

I know the LORD is always with me.
I will not be shaken, for he is right beside me.

Psalm 16:8
New Living Translation

The LORD is my light and my salvation;
whom shall I fear?
the LORD is the strength of my life;
of whom shall I be afraid?

Psalm 27:1
King James Version

He is our God,
    we are his people

Come, let us praise the LORD!
Let us sing for joy to God, who protects us!
Let us come before him with thanksgiving
and sing joyful songs of praise.
For the LORD is a mighty God,
a mighty king over all the gods.
He rules over the whole earth,
from the deepest caves to the highest hills.
He rules over the sea, which he made;
the land also, which he himself formed.
Come, let us bow down and worship him;
let us kneel before the LORD, our Maker!
He is our God; we are the people he cares for,
the flock for which he provides.

Psalm 95:1–7
Good News Translation

Judean Wilderness

He deserves our praise

Praise the LORD!

Praise God in his sanctuary!
Praise him in his heavens for his acts of power!
Praise him for his mighty acts!
Praise him according to his excellent greatness!
Praise him with the sounding of the trumpet!
Praise him with harp and lyre!
Praise him with tambourine and dancing!
Praise him with stringed instruments and flute!
Praise him with loud cymbals!
Praise him with resounding cymbals!

Psalm 150:1-5
World English Bible

Normandy Sunset